MW01152554

To Skyler & Colin ♡

With LOVE...

Carole Stevens Bibisi

and Miss American Bronte...

Copyright © 2007 by Carole Stevens Bibisi

ISBN: 1-59849-026-5
Library of Congress Control Number: 2006936154
Printed in China

Contact me through my website www.ArtHarmonyCSB.com
What are your favorite pages? Send me your drawings of American Bronte.
I used colored pencils and markers to create this book.
My cat Bronte supervised and inspired me to create her story.

All rights reserved. No part of this book may be transmitted in any form or
by any means, electronic or mechanical, including photocopying, recording,
or by any information storage or retrieval system, without the written
permission of the publisher, except where permitted by law.

Peanut Butter Publishing
2925 Fairview Avenue East
Seattle, Washington 98102
877-728-8837
info@peanutbutterpublishing.com

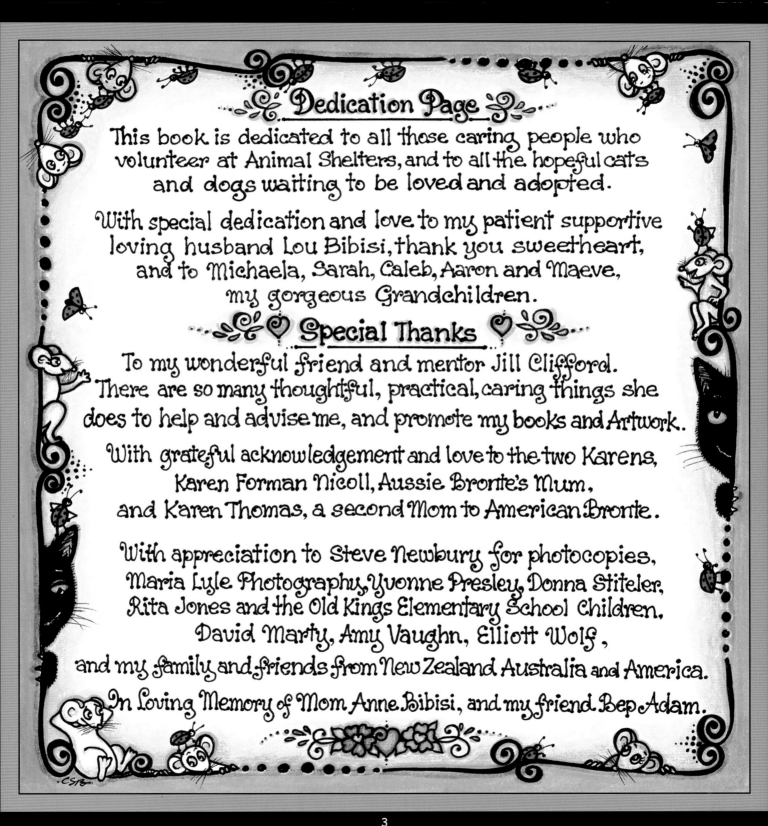

Dedication Page

This book is dedicated to all those caring people who volunteer at Animal Shelters, and to all the hopeful cats and dogs waiting to be loved and adopted.

With special dedication and love to my patient supportive loving husband Lou Bibisi, thank you sweetheart, and to Michaela, Sarah, Caleb, Aaron and Maeve, my gorgeous Grandchildren.

Special Thanks

To my wonderful friend and mentor Jill Clifford. There are so many thoughtful, practical, caring things she does to help and advise me, and promote my books and Artwork.

With grateful acknowledgement and love to the two Karens, Karen Forman Nicoll, Aussie Bronte's Mum, and Karen Thomas, a second Mom to American Bronte.

With appreciation to Steve Newbury for photocopies, Maria Lyle Photography, Yvonne Presley, Donna Stiteler, Rita Jones and the Old Kings Elementary School Children, David Marty, Amy Vaughn, Elliott Wolf, and my family and friends from New Zealand Australia and America.

In Loving Memory of Mom Anne Bibisi, and my friend Bep Adam.

I'm American Bronte,
pronounced Bron-tee.
I'm the coolest of cats
you'll have to agree.
I'm black and beautiful
with a
pedigree,
and I live in
💙America
the land of the
free!

On the other side of the world
in a land down under....
lives the old black cat I was named after.
Compared to me, she's antique fur.
Australian Bronte's
just an
amateur!

AMERICA

AUSTRALIA

NEW ZEALAND

Down Under

I'm a black cat,
full of mystery and intrigue....
A witches cat on a broomstick
traveling at speed.
I'm especially popular on Halloween night.
It's 'trick or treat' in the bright moonlight.

I'm under the bed again, I'm hiding here.
My humans are looking for me everywhere.
They didn't think that I could s-q-u-e-e-z-e

dust bunnies

under such a low bed, but I did it with ease.

CSB.

I love Mom's potted plants
in the big patio too.
I rearrange the dirt for her....
Whoop-de-do!

It's my duty of course,
so why hesitate?
I must help my
humans
redecorate!

It's no use giving me food in a dish,
I like to play in it, and make it squish
all over the carpet and the tiled floor.
I'm so helpful to the humans
I love and adore!

They've got this exciting play thing. It jumps around like a big spring. They move the stick with a flick of the wrist.

I just have to chase it—

I can't resist!

I used to crawl under
the sheet
and pounce every time
they moved their feet.
My humans couldn't sleep
so they kicked me out.
"Go to sleep in your own bed,
now Bronte, don't pout."

I like to jump on my Mom's desk,
I'm not really trying to be a pest,
but Mom's too busy to play with me,
so I shake fur on her
artwork and Pootry

Mom's closet is such
an exciting place, with
corners to hide in
and lots of space.
I can see Mom,
but she can't see me.
She's looking for her
'darling' girl
Bronte.

There's lots of clothes
and shoes and stuff—
handbags, boxes and
bits of fluff.
Those dust-bunnies twitch
and tremble in fear.
I sneeze and make
them disappear!

Suitcases? What? You're starting to pack?
I think I'm having a panic attack.
Mom and Dad, don't go! Please stay!
Take me with you — or I'll stowaway!